SEE AMERICAN HISTORY

# THE
# CIVIL WAR

1861–1865

*The Art of*

## MORT KÜNSTLER

*Text by*

## JAMES I. ROBERTSON, JR.

★

### ABBEVILLE KIDS

A DIVISION OF ABBEVILLE PRESS

New York   London

*In memory of Leon Friend, my art teacher at Abraham Lincoln High School in Brooklyn, whose teachings influence me to this day.*

Front and back cover: Union and Confederate soldiers fight at Gettysburg. See page 30.
Frontispiece: Troops prepare for the Battle of Fredericksburg. See page 20.
Back endpaper: Confederate forces arrive at Bull Run. See page 10.

Editor: Nicole Lanctot
Designer: Misha Beletsky
Composition: Ada Rodriguez
Production manager: Louise Kurtz

First edition
1 3 5 7 9 10 8 6 4 2

ISBN 978-0-7892-1252-8

Library of Congress Cataloging-in-Publication Data available upon request

For bulk or premium sales and for text adoption procedures, write to Customer Service Manager, 116 West 23rd Street, New York, NY 10011, or call 1-800-ARTBOOK.

Visit Abbeville Press online at www.abbeville.com.

# TABLE OF CONTENTS

*The Story of the Civil War* ............................................ 6

*The Fall of Fort Sumter — The Civil War Begins ★ 1861* ... 8

*The First Battle of Bull Run ★ 1861* ............................... 10

*Clash of the Ironclads ★ 1862* ..................................... 12

*Jackson Enters Winchester, Virginia ★ 1862* ................... 14

*The Second Battle of Bull Run and the
   Battle of Antietam ★ 1862* ....................................... 16

*The Emancipation Proclamation ★ 1862–1863* ............... 18

*Battle of Fredericksburg ★ 1862* ................................. 20

*Angel of the Battlefield ★ 1862* .................................. 22

*Battle of Chancellorsville ★ 1863* ............................... 24

*Gettysburg: Day One ★ 1863* ..................................... 26

*Gettysburg: Day Two ★ 1863* ..................................... 28

*Gettysburg: Day Three ★ 1863* ................................... 30

*Vicksburg Victory ★ 1863* ......................................... 32

*Lincoln Speaks, Grant Triumphs ★ 1863* ...................... 34

*The Doomed Voyage of CSS* Hunley *★ 1864* ................. 36

*On to Richmond! ★ 1864* .......................................... 38

*Atlanta Burns ★ 1864* .............................................. 40

*Lee Surrenders ★ 1865* ............................................. 42

TIMELINE ................................................................ 44

KEY PEOPLE ............................................................ 45

# The Story of the Civil War

For the first decades of the United States, our country's leaders argued over two major problems. The first one was slavery, and the second one was the limited power that the states had in the new union. By the 1840s, people debated not only about slavery but whether new territories in the West would become "free" or "slave" states. Meanwhile, thousands of immigrants were pouring into the North. A huge industrial revolution was turning the North into a major producer of goods. These developments threatened the economic hold that the cotton planters of the South had long enjoyed. Prosperity there came through the free labor of slaves in the field. Soon, emotions grew out of control, and people on both sides felt they had to act.

In December 1860, South Carolina decided to separate from the Union. Six other southern states—Mississippi, Florida, Alabama, Georgia, Louisiana, and Texas—followed South Carolina. The creation of the Confederate States of America came in February 1861. Two months later, Confederate forces at Charleston bombarded the Union-held Fort Sumter. The firing on the fort was the last straw in a long series of small events that became too much for people to handle.

The immediate cause of the war was secession—the states leaving the Union. The southern states believed that they had voluntarily joined the United States, so they felt that they could just as voluntarily leave. Abraham Lincoln (ABOVE), barely a month in office as president of the United States, felt strongly the other way. Lincoln's call for troops after Fort Sumter led four other states (Virginia, Arkansas, Tennessee, and North Carolina) to join with their southern relations.

For two years, preservation of the Union was the goal of the northern forces. Then, in 1863, with the Emancipation Proclamation, ending slavery became a second major issue in the struggle for the United States.

At first, it seemed that the Civil War would only be one battle, lasting six months at most. The Union was well-established, with a functioning Congress and president, federal agencies, a flag, and American traditions. Confederate leaders had to start over to create their new country. This Confederacy had no armies or naval power. No foreign powers gave it recognition or encouragement.

The Union had a manpower base of twenty-two million people who could fight. The Confederacy had only 5.5 million citizens for soldiers. Thanks to the ongoing industrial revolution, there were single states in the North that produced more goods than the entire South.

Geography also played a role in the war. The Confederacy was an area the size of Western Europe. It had the Appalachian Mountains and a 3,000-mile coastline, which was a major problem for the Union navy.

In addition, there were two real advantages the Confederacy enjoyed at the start of the war. More southerners had made the army a career, and Confederate generals were more skilled than their Union counterparts. More importantly, Union soldiers had to leave home to invade the South. Confederate armies were defending their homes and families. Twenty-five percent of southerners owned slaves, but fighting to preserve their way of life in general was as important as life itself.

The Battle of Appomattox Court House was not the end of the Civil War, but it was the beginning of the end. In 1865, Lincoln was a friend to the South because of his negotiation efforts, but he was murdered only five days after Lee's surrender. The political fight that followed in the U.S. Congress lasted three times longer than the actual war. It brought Reconstruction and military occupation of the South, along with resistance to providing full civil rights to African Americans for one hundred years. On the other hand, the Civil War led to the settlement of the West. Thirty-five years later, a unified United States became the greatest industrial nation in the world.

The struggle of the 1860s is often called "the first modern war" because it brought forth a number of new items to warfare: rifles (rather than inaccurate muskets), hand grenades, machine guns, an ambulance network, ironclad naval vessels, and many other revolutionary changes.

Many famous Americans that we still know today appeared in the Civil War: Abraham Lincoln, Robert E. Lee, Ulysses S. Grant, Stonewall Jackson, William T. Sherman, and Jefferson Davis, among others. We also cannot forget the three million everyday people who fought for what they believed in. Now, 150 years later, we still marvel at their courage, willpower, and sacrifice.

The United States that we know today was born in 1865, at the end of the Civil War. History is the best teacher we will ever have: By remembering the deeds of the past, Americans can learn to be even prouder of our nation.

# The Fall of Fort Sumter — The Civil War Begins

★1861

On December 20, 1860, South Carolina separated from the United States, which was just seventy-two years old. Six other states followed South Carolina, and together they created the Confederate States of

America. At the time, South Carolina's Fort Sumter was occupied by the United States army, also called the Union. When the Confederates demanded that Fort Sumter be surrendered, the new Union president, Abraham Lincoln, refused. The quiet dawn of April 12, 1861, was broken when more than seventy cannon opened fire on Fort Sumter from the north, west, and south.

Confederate general P. G. T. Beauregard (ABOVE) ordered the first shot on Fort Sumter. See the cannon's smoke and the sky lit up by the red flames of battle?

The bombardment continued all day, all night, and halfway through the next day. Some 4,000 shells crashed into the brick walls of the fort. The eighty-six Union soldiers were helpless. Nevertheless, Sgt. John Carmody (LEFT) at one point decided on his own to reply to the Confederate artillery fire. Carmody rushed to the guns and fired every loaded cannon he found. The three stripes on his shoulder identify him as a sergeant, and their red color shows that he is an artilleryman. The rope he pulls, called a lanyard, fires the cannon.

The fort was in flames. With his troops out of food and ammunition, the Union major Robert Anderson surrendered. President Lincoln called for 75,000 volunteer soldiers to respond to this attack against the Union and the federal government. Four more states separated from the Union because they did not want to volunteer troops. So it began—the bloodiest war in American history.

# The First Battle of Bull Run

## ★1861

General Irvin McDowell of the Union knew very little about battle, and neither did the 30,000 blue uniformed soldiers he led into Virginia. His force advanced thirty miles to the village of Manassas, located near a creek called Bull Run. McDowell attacked Confederate forces on a hot Sunday. Large numbers of nearby Washington, DC, residents traveled to Bull Run to watch the battle. They even brought picnic lunches! It was expected that the Union army would quickly end the Confederate uprising.

A Confederate force waited in battle lines. One brigade, led by a college professor named Thomas Jackson (ABOVE), had come by train from the Shenandoah Valley to strengthen the Confederate army.

Both generals fought desperately through the morning. The Union forces were about to break the enemy line when General Jackson's soldiers secured a hilltop and stopped the advance. Another Confederate general rallied his men by shouting, "Look! There stands Jackson like a stone wall!" Jackson's actions won the day, and they brought him the most famous nickname in American military history.

"Stonewall" Jackson was a strange sight that day. His Virginians were dressed in Confederate gray, while he wore the blue uniform of a Virginia Military Institute teacher (LEFT). His horse was not as large as others, but Little Sorrel was swift and obedient. Do you see the official flag of the Confederates behind Stonewall Jackson?

# Clash of the Ironclads

★1862

On March 9, two strange warships locked in battle at Hampton Roads in the harbor of Norfolk, Virginia. Powered entirely by steam engines and unlike any other warships in history, they were

plated with iron (LEFT). In the painting, see the bigger of the "ironclads," called CSS *Virginia*, flying the Confederate flag? It had iron plates covering its sides. It was built to sink the wooden ships of the U.S. Navy.

See the smaller ship in front of the CSS *Virginia*? It is the USS *Monitor*. The Union had built it to destroy the wooden warships of the Confederate navy. Although the *Virginia* was larger and carried more guns, it was so slow that it took a whole hour for the ship to turn around. The *Monitor*, on the other hand, was faster and more difficult to hit with gunfire. This was because so little of the ship floated above the water; it was almost like a submarine. It had a rotating turret with two guns, so Union gunners could turn it to shoot in every direction.

The USS *Monitor* steamed into the harbor. The CSS *Virginia* had already sunk two wooden warships and forced a third, the USS *Minnesota,* to run aground. After four hours of pounding one another with cannonballs, both vessels were damaged, yet neither could sink the other! Still, these newer, stronger ships set an example for every other navy in the world. Instead of simple wooden warships, the age of great ironclad warships had begun.

A month before this meeting, Confederate general Nathan Bedford Forrest (RIGHT) had led cavalry—a group of soldiers on horseback—to fight against Union soldiers in the Battle of Shiloh in Tennessee.

# Jackson Enters Winchester, Virginia

★1862

Midmorning on May 25, Jackson's forces broke the Union lines south of Winchester, in Virginia. The Union troops ran through town and toward the Potomac River, like a group of "disorganized fugitives," Jackson reported. The Confederates then marched through Winchester victoriously. Children gave gifts to the troops passing through. What is the boy handing to Stonewall in the picture (RIGHT)? Do you see what kind of fruit the girl is giving to a soldier (BELOW)?

# The Second Battle of Bull Run and the Battle of Antietam

## ★1862

At the 1861 First Battle of Bull Run, Stonewall Jackson had told his men to "yell like Furies," to sound like demons coming at Union soldiers. From then on, the "rebel yell," as it was called, became a fearful announcement that the Confederates were attacking.

The yell was heard several times during the Second Battle of Bull Run (August 28–30). Confederate general Robert E. Lee was outnumbered almost two to one by Union general John Pope's 75,000 troops. Lee's success came from sending Stonewall Jackson and his men on a wide march around the end of Pope's troop line—his "flank." This gave Lee the advantage of attacking from two directions at the same time. Of course, you cannot actually *hear* the rebel yell in this picture, but can you *see* the men doing it (ABOVE RIGHT)? Having cleared

Virginia of two major Union armies, Lee decided to invade northern territory. A victory on northern soil might convince the Union to end the war — and let the Confederate States of America have its independence. Lee's army got as far as Sharpsburg, Maryland. There, on September 17, along the banks of Antietam Creek, occurred the bloodiest single day of battle in our nation's history. Each side fought savagely through cornfields, woods, and open fields. In the first three hours of the battle, Jackson's Confederates showed why they were called the Stonewall brigade. When nightfall brought an end to the contest, some 23,000 men had been killed or wounded — in just thirteen hours of fighting.

In this picture (RIGHT), see Jackson on his horse. What can he be thinking with so many of his men lying wounded around him?

# The Emancipation Proclamation
## ★1862–1863

As Lee retreated to Virginia, President Lincoln (LEFT) made his most historic decision. He believed that the North and the South could not be reunited until slavery was eliminated from the land.

Lincoln wanted to issue an emancipation order—a statement freeing someone from slavery—from a position of strength, not weakness. Although the Battle of Antietam was not a clear victory, it had ended with Lee's army leaving Union territory. Five days after the battle, the president issued the Preliminary Emancipation Proclamation. It warned the Confederacy that slaves living in areas still "in rebellion"—that is, still fighting against the United States—on January 1, 1863, would be free forever. It was an opening step toward freedom for all Americans. Just as important, the Proclamation allowed African Americans to join Union armies and strengthen the fight for reuniting the country.

The Emancipation Proclamation was temporary. To make it permanent meant changing (amending) the Constitution. The Thirteenth Amendment to outlaw slavery forever in the United States was passed by the required two-thirds vote on January 31, 1865. A huge celebration followed. The 54th Massachusetts Infantry (ABOVE) became the first African American regiment to fight for the Union.

# Battle of Fredericksburg

★1862

The success of the Emancipation Proclamation depended on how effective Union armies could be in the field. Union general George McClellan's decision not to pursue Lee's army after Antietam gave Lincoln no choice: He had to find another commander who could fight successfully. He chose General Ambrose Burnside. The Rhode Island general sought to get around Lee's army and force a battle. Unfortunately, when Burnside crossed the Rappahannock River with troops at Fredericksburg, Lee (LEFT, with the gray beard) and General James Longstreet were waiting for them on the hills behind the town. On December 12, Union soldiers advanced across open ground an astounding thirteen times against Confederate artillery and infantrymen. And thirteen times the Union army was thrown back, with heavy losses.

Colonel Joshua Chamberlain and his 20th Maine regiment were in one of the final assaults (BELOW). The survivors of the assault spent the night lying on the field; they even used dead men as shields against the heavy fire.

# Angel of the Battlefield
### ★1862

Many wounded men needed care after the fighting, and civilians volunteered to help. Two of the most famous are seen in this painting (LEFT). Clara Barton, called "the Angel of the Battlefield," pours a cup of soup. After the war, she established the American Red Cross. Another volunteer nurse was the great American poet Walt Whitman. He is the gray-bearded man with a green scarf, holding a canteen to a wounded man's lips. Can you spot him?

A month after the defeat at Fredericksburg, Burnside began a march up the Rappahannock River to surprise the Confederates from behind. During his travel, three days of icy rain created treacherous, knee-deep mud, as you can see (ABOVE).

# Battle of Chancellorsville

★1863

Lincoln thought that he had picked a winner when he chose General "Fighting Joe" Hooker to replace the bumbling Burnside. Hooker started well. He rebuilt the Union Army of the Potomac and gave it all the supplies it needed. He raised morale to a new level, drew up a solid battle plan, and promised his commander in chief: "May God have mercy on General Lee, for I will have none."

Hooker split his army of 134,000 men into two parts. He positioned them so that he could squeeze Lee like a gigantic pair of pliers. But at a critical point, Hooker unfortunately paused. Lee quickly took the offensive. He boldly split his small force into *three* segments and sent the largest—under Jackson—to sweep again around the flank of the Union army. Jackson's attack caught the soldiers off guard. From May 1 to 6, Confederates pounded Union positions at every point. Hooker's 17,000 losses were worse than what Burnside suffered at Fredericksburg.

At the height of the Chancellorsville fighting, Lee rode victoriously through the Confederate ranks. Can you see the soldiers cheering for Lee (LEFT)? Writers have called this impossible victory "the most supreme moment in Lee's life." But Chancellorsville came at a great cost to Lee. Among his losses was Stonewall Jackson himself, who was accidentally shot by his own men in the confusion of combat. The body of the thirty-nine-year-old general was taken to the Virginia Military Institute and placed in his old classroom before burial the next day. Can you spot Stonewall Jackson's wife, Anna, dressed in black behind the coffin (ABOVE)? No other personal loss in the war hit the Confederates harder than the death of Stonewall Jackson.

# Gettysburg: Day One

★1863

The stunning victory at Chancellorsville convinced Lee that a second raid into Union territory was the best strategy to take. It would move the fighting out of Virginia and the South, which had been hit hard. As his soldiers traveled north, the raid would allow Lee to gather needed food from the rich fields of Pennsylvania. A battle in northern territory would

also strengthen the wish for peace in the Union states. And if Lee could defeat Hooker's army again, as he had done in Virginia, the door would be open for an easy advance on Washington, DC, itself.

A week into the campaign, things began to go wrong for Lee. His army filed across the Potomac River, with General James Johnston Pettigrew's well-known soldiers from North Carolina setting the pace.

However, Lee's cavalry chief "Jeb" Stuart went looking for Union supply trains. Because his mounted horsemen were not there to lead the way and provide information, Lee could not keep informed of Union army movements.

Meanwhile, Hooker's slowness in pursuing Lee and his habit of arguing with superiors led to his replacement. General George Meade took command of the Union army only three days before one of the major battles of the war exploded in Meade's state of Pennsylvania.

Union cavalry met up with Confederate infantry at a small town called Gettysburg. Union horsemen under General John Buford (LEFT) were outnumbered in the fighting on July 1. They held their ground for valuable hours until Union troops were rushed to Gettysburg. By nightfall, Confederates held the town. Meade's army was taking positions on Cemetery Ridge, a long and narrow strip of land. Can you see the fence and rocks they used to defend themselves (ABOVE)? On the end of the strip of land were two prominent hills: Little Round Top and Big Round Top.

# Gettysburg: Day Two

★1863

On July 2, Lee attacked both ends of the Union line, but without success. Many acts of bravery marked the action. One example was the bravery of the 20th Maine, led by Col. Lawrence Chamberlain, a former college professor. Can you see their bayonets (LEFT and ABOVE)? They were like sharp knives attached to the ends of the rifles. The regiment beat back a number of attacks against Little Round Top. When the troops ran out of ammunition, the New Englanders charged with

their bayonets, but acted as if they were fully armed. Their exhausted opponents retreated from the hill. General Jeb Stuart (LEFT, holding his hat) returned late on July 2 to Lee's headquarters, too late to be of any real help.

# Gettysburg: Day Three

★1863

The climax of Gettysburg came on the third day of battle. Earlier tries had shown that the flanks of the Union army could not be broken. Lee decided instead to launch an assault on the Union center. For two hours, the heaviest canon fire of the entire war took place. Then, at 3 p.m., some 13,000 Confederates under General George Pickett started across a big field toward the heavily fortified Union line.

"Pickett's Charge" (LEFT) lasted forty minutes. It was a disaster for the Confederate army. The attack failed not from a lack of bravery—there was plenty of that. See, for instance, General Lewis Armistead proudly leading his Virginia brigade with his hat on top of a raised sword (RIGHT). The Confederate effort was simply blown to pieces by intense musket and cannon fire. Over half of the Confederates who fought were killed or wounded. Of Pickett's three brigade commanders, two were killed, and the third man was badly wounded. All thirteen regimental colonels in the charge died in the action. Survivors who staggered back to the Confederate lines found Lee waiting for them and saying, "It is all my fault. . . . It is I who have lost the battle."

More than 51,000 casualties at Gettysburg made the name of the town immortal. On July 4, the Union army was too bloodied and too weary to celebrate the nation's birthday. That day, Lee placed his wounded men in wagons that made a train twelve miles long. In the steady rain, they began the painful march back to Virginia.

# Vicksburg Victory

★1863

In 1861, the Mississippi River, which runs down the length of the United States from north to south, was like a busy highway for soldiers and supplies. Control of the river fell slowly into Union hands. By late 1862, Confederates held onto a small stretch of the waterway in Mississippi and Louisiana. Its main defense was Vicksburg, Mississippi, a town nestled on high hills overlooking a huge curve in the river. Confederates turned this spot into a powerful fortress.

The greatest trait of Union general Ulysses S. Grant was his determination. If he set out to achieve a goal, he would not sway from it—he never gave up. For eight months Grant tried to take Vicksburg. He finally was able to surround the city. Outside help could not get into the town, and those in town were trapped and driven to starvation. On July 4 (Independence Day), Vicksburg collapsed. Grant rode into the city like the conquering hero he was (ABOVE RIGHT). "The Father of Waters," Lincoln exclaimed, "runs unvexed [unbothered] to the sea."

Twin losses at Gettysburg and Vicksburg crippled Confederate morale. However, there were independent cavalry leaders who ranged far afield on raids. The best-known of these Confederate raiders was Kentucky's John Hunt Morgan. In July 1863, Morgan took 2,400 cavalry on a spectacular ride through Kentucky and Ohio. The men destroyed bridges, burned warehouses, and released prisoners. They also looted homes and frightened innocent citizens. Morgan's "Ohio Raid" (LEFT) ended in failure, however, with Morgan himself thrown into prison like a common criminal.

# Lincoln Speaks, Grant Triumphs

## ★1863

An emotional ceremony occurred on November 19, 1863, at Gettysburg. Seventeen acres of battlefield had been set aside as a soldiers' cemetery, and fifteen thousand people were present for the event. President Lincoln was not the first speaker, and had in fact been asked to make just "a few appropriate remarks." His 272 words now have a sacred place in American literature and history: His short speech is known as the Gettysburg Address.

Lincoln spoke of the freedom and equality everyone should have. He praised the dead soldiers who had given "the last full measure of devotion" to their country. The Union "shall not perish from the earth," he promised.

While Lincoln was at Gettysburg, Grant's Union army was moving against the last Confederate stronghold in the western theater:

Chattanooga, Tennessee. On November 24, three Union divisions moved slowly up the steep face of Lookout Mountain (RIGHT), which rises 1,400 feet above the valley floor. Fog, drizzle, and smoke covered the rocky slope. When the sky cleared and the gunfire ended, the Stars and Stripes waved on the mountaintop. Grant had triumphed again.

# The Doomed Voyage of CSS *Hunley*

★1864

Horace Hunley had a dream: to build a submarine for the Confederates that could sink ships twenty times its size. For two years he developed a forty-foot vessel (RIGHT) powered by a seven-man crew, who would turn a long shaft connected to the propeller. On the front of the strange-looking boat was a long beam called a "spar." Can you spot the spar attached to the front of the boat at the bottom of the picture? At the end of it was a harpoon-like spear and a barrel of explosives. The submarine's goal was to ram an enemy ship, and then pull away. When it had moved away, the crew would pull a rope that would start an explosion — and sink the enemy ship!

Twenty-one men died during many test trials. The painting shows the crew preparing for a mission on the night of February 17, 1864. George Dixon, the submarine's commander, looks at his pocket watch, checking when the tide is going out so the submarine can go out with it. The CSS *Hunley* set off from its pier at Charleston, South Carolina. The submarine rammed the warship USS *Housatonic*, and the Union ship sank in a matter of minutes. CSS *Hunley* was not seen again until 1994, when divers found it half-buried in the harbor. The submarine, the first underwater craft ever to sink an enemy ship in combat, also managed to sink itself. It is now being restored in Charleston.

# On to Richmond!

★1864

Since the war's start, President Lincoln had picked one general after another to lead the Union's armies. One after the other, they all had failed. Finally, Lincoln chose Ulysses S. Grant, the man who had captured Vicksburg, Mississippi.

Grant's plan was to march to Richmond, Virginia—the capital of the Confederacy. He knew that Robert E. Lee would try to stop him. Each time Lee tried, Grant intended to wear down his army by fighting it, again and again. Eventually, the Army of Northern Virginia would be too worn out to fight anymore.

The march to Richmond was called the Overland Campaign. It lasted from May 4 to June 24, 1864, and consisted of twelve separate battles. The first one was the Battle of the Wilderness, where Grant lost more men than Lee. But he kept marching on. Grant (LEFT) looks determined as his men cheer for him the night after the hard battle. How do you think Grant felt when he heard his men cheer?

At Spotsylvania Court House, the site of the next battle, Grant again lost more men than Lee. One corner of the battlefield was called the "Bloody Angle" (RIGHT) because the fighting there was so fierce. But the Union had more men than the Confederacy. Grant had a bigger army than Lee. Grant could replace his losses; Lee could not. No matter how many men Grant lost, he kept marching "on to Richmond!"

# Atlanta Burns

★1864

During the Civil War, railroads moved soldiers and supplies over long distances. In the Confederacy, the main railroads crossed in Atlanta, Georgia. Grant ordered one of his best generals, William T. Sherman, to capture Atlanta and destroy this Confederate railroad hub.

Sherman's Atlanta Campaign began in May and ended on September 2, 1864, after the railroad lines were cut and the Confederate army had left the city. Six days later, General Sherman ordered all civilian (non-soldier) residents to leave, too. The mayor and city council wrote him a letter, begging him to let the people stay. Sherman said no. "The only way the people of Atlanta can hope once more to live in peace and quiet at home," he replied, "is to stop the war."

Weeks later, on November 11, Sherman ordered his men to destroy "everything of military significance" in Atlanta. When Sherman marched out of Atlanta on November 16, he left behind a burning ruin (RIGHT).

While Sherman destroyed the Confederacy's main railroad hub,

another Union general, Philip Sheridan, chased Confederate raider Jubal Early. On October 19, Early had made a surprise attack on Union forces at Cedar Creek, Virginia. Miles away at the time, Sheridan rode hard to the battlefield on his magnificent jet-black horse named Rienzi (LEFT). He was just in time to lead a successful counterattack. News of Sheridan's victory, together with Sherman's capture of Atlanta, helped Lincoln get elected again in November 1864.

# Lee Surrenders

## ★1865

No war of such violence ever ended on more peaceable terms. Grant stopped the ten-month attack on Lee's army on April 2 with an all-out fight that overwhelmed the little Confederate army. Some 25,000

Confederate soldiers (about a third of the army's normal size) staggered westward in retreat. Grant's soldiers swarmed around and finally surrounded the Confederates.

On a chilly Palm Sunday, Lee (LEFT, on his horse) and Grant (holding his hat) met at a home in Appomattox, Virginia. The Confederate general could have avoided such humiliation by ordering his men to fight for as long as it took the Union soldiers to get tired and quit. But Lee said no: such a course would leave scars that would forever prevent the North and South from becoming one country again.

Grant also had a choice. He could have tried and hanged Confederate officials, put others in jail, and treated former Confederate soldiers as criminals. Grant said no: It was time to put anger aside and get on with the business of rebuilding a damaged country. Ex-Confederates could go home quietly. As long as they obeyed the laws, they would not be disturbed.

On that day, April 9, two American generals served their country well. Northerners returned home with victory; southerners went home with dignity.

Grant and Lee exchanged salutes, and the Confederates surrendered their arms (ABOVE). This respectful meeting was the first permanent step on the road to a new and stronger Union.

# ★ The Civil War: Timeline

## 1860

November 6: Abraham Lincoln is elected president.

December 20: South Carolina becomes the first state to secede.

## 1861

February 4: The Confederate States of America is formed.

April 13: Fort Sumter in Charleston Harbor surrenders to Confederate forces. The Civil War begins.

July 21: The Confederate army wins the First Battle of Manassas (or First Bull Run).

## 1862

February 6: Union general Ulysses S. Grant captures Fort Henry on the Tennessee River.

March 9: U.S. Navy ironclad *Monitor* battles the Confederacy's ironclad *Virginia*.

April 6–7: Ulysses S. Grant wins the Battle of Shiloh in Tennessee.

April 25: Union naval commander David G. Farragut captures New Orleans, Louisiana.

May 31–June 1: Union general George B. McClellan is halted at the Battle of Seven Pines.

June 8–9: Jackson wins the 1862 Valley Campaign with victories at Cross Keys and Port Republic.

June 25–July 1: Confederate general Robert E. Lee defeats Union general George B. McClellan in the "Seven Days Battles."

August 28–30: General Lee defeats Union general John Pope at the Second Battle of Manassas, Virginia (or Bull Run).

September 17: Union general George B. McClellan achieves a victory against Robert E. Lee at the Battle of Antietam near Sharpsburg, Maryland.

September 22: President Lincoln issues the preliminary Emancipation Proclamation.

December 13: Lee defeats the Union army at Fredericksburg, Virginia.

## 1863

January 1: Lincoln's Emancipation Proclamation takes effect.

May 1–6: Robert E. Lee defeats "Fighting Joe" Hooker at the Battle of Chancellorsville, Virginia.

July 1–3: The Union Army of the Potomac defeats the Confederate Army of Northern Virginia at the Battle of Gettysburg.

July 2–26: Confederate John Hunt Morgan leads a 1,000-mile raid through Ohio.

July 4: Union general Ulysses S. Grant captures Vicksburg, Mississippi.

July 18: Union colonel Robert Gould Shaw leads the 54th Massachusetts, the first African American regiment, in an assault on Fort Wagner, South Carolina.

September 19–20: Confederates win the Battle of Chickamauga in Georgia, forcing Union general William Rosecrans to retreat to Chattanooga, Tennessee.

November 25–27: The Union wins the Chattanooga Campaign.

# 1864

February 17: The submarine CSS *Hunley* sinks the USS *Housatonic*.

May 4–June 24: Ulysses S. Grant drives Robert E. Lee to Richmond in the Overland Campaign.

July 11: Confederate general Jubal A. Early attacks Fort Stevens, on the edge of Washington, DC.

August 5: Union rear admiral David Farragut wins the Battle of Mobile Bay, Alabama, capturing the last Confederate port on the Gulf of Mexico.

September 2: General William Tecumseh Sherman captures Atlanta, Georgia.

November 8: Abraham Lincoln is reelected.

November 15–December 21: Sherman rides out of Atlanta, leading a "March to the Sea."

November 30: Union forces win the Battle of Franklin, Tennessee.

December 15–16: Union forces win the Battle of Nashville, Tennessee.

December 21: Sherman captures Savannah, Georgia.

# 1865

April 3: Union forces occupy Richmond, Virginia.

April 9: Robert E. Lee surrenders to Ulysses S. Grant at Appomattox, Virginia.

April 14: John Wilkes Booth shoots President Abraham Lincoln.

April 15: Andrew Johnson becomes the seventeenth president of the United States.

April 26: Joseph E. Johnston surrenders the Confederate Army at Bennett.

# ★ Key People

Barton, Clara (1821–1912) · Called the "Angel of the Battlefield," Barton was a volunteer nurse who later (in 1881) founded the American Red Cross.

Beauregard, P. G. T. (1818–1893) · Confederate General. Commander of the assault on Fort Sumter, he was a general at the First Battle of Bull Run and commanded the Army of Mississippi at Shiloh.

Buford, John (1826–1863) · Union Major General. As a cavalry division commander he held off a major Confederate force long enough to prevent a Union defeat on day one of the Battle of Gettysburg.

Burnside, Ambrose E. (1824–1881) · Union Major General. Burnside commanded the Army of the Potomac at Fredericksburg, where he suffered a terrible defeat.

Davis, Jefferson (1808–1889) · Davis was the first and last president of the Confederate States of America.

Farragut, David G. (1801–1870) · Union Vice Admiral. Farragut led the capture of both New Orleans and Mobile Bay.

Grant, Ulysses S. (1822–1885) · Union General. Grant attracted the notice of President Lincoln by proving himself a winning general early in the war. In 1864, Lincoln chose him as general in chief of Union armies. He led the Union to final victory.

Hood, John Bell (1831–1879) · Confederate Lt. General. A bold but reckless commander, Hood lost Atlanta to General William T. Sherman, and his Army of Tennessee was soundly defeated by General George H. Thomas at the Battle of Nashville.

**Hooker, Joseph ("Fighting Joe") (1814–1879)** · Union Major General. Hooker was named commanding officer of Army of the Potomac after the Battle of Fredericksburg, but he was badly defeated by Robert E. Lee at Chancellorsville.

**Jackson, Thomas J. ("Stonewall") (1824–1863)** · Confederate Lt. General. One of the most famous generals of the Civil War, Jackson was a hero of the First Battle of Manassas and went on to command the Shenandoah Valley Campaign. He was accidentally shot by his own troops at the Battle of Chancellorsville and later died of his wounds.

**Johnson, Andrew (1808–1875)** · Lincoln's vice president, he became the seventeenth U.S. president on the death of Lincoln.

**Johnston, Joseph E. (1807–1891)** · Confederate General. Johnston was a top commander at the First Battle of Manassas. He surrendered the Army of Tennessee to General Sherman at the end of the war.

**Lee, Robert E. (1807–1870)** · Confederate General. The most widely admired general in the Civil War, Lee commanded the Army of Northern Virginia—the principal army of the Confederacy.

**Lincoln, Abraham (1809–1865)** · Sixteenth president of the United States, Lincoln led the Union through the Civil War until his assassination on April 14, 1865.

**McClellan, George B. (1826–1885)** · Union Major General. Known as the "Young Napoleon," McClellan commanded the Army of the Potomac until November 1862.

**McDowell, Irvin (1818–1885)** · Union Major General. Defeated at the First Battle of Bull Run.

**Meade, George Gordon (1815–1872)** · Union Major General. Meade led the Army of the Potomac to victory at Gettysburg and commanded that army through the end of the war.

**Morgan, John Hunt (1825–1864)** · Confederate Brigadier General. A master of guerrilla warfare, Morgan led raids in Kentucky and Ohio.

**Pickett, George E. (1825–1875)** · Confederate Major General. Pickett commanded the division that attacked Union forces during the final day at Gettysburg.

**Pope, John (1822–1892)** · Union Major General. An experienced commander, Pope was defeated at the Second Battle of Manassas.

**Sheridan, Philip H. (1831–1888)** · Union Major General. "Little Phil" was the Union's leading cavalry officer.

**Sherman, William Tecumseh (1820–1891)** · Union Major General. Sherman was General Grant's right-hand man. He captured Atlanta and did great damage to Georgia during his "March to the Sea." He captured Savannah, Georgia, and won some of the war's final battles in the Carolinas.

**Thomas, George H. (1816–1870)** · Union General who earned the nickname "Rock of Chickamauga."